Why Men Fart and Women Pick Flowers

Sophie Middlemiss

CROMBIE JARDINE
Publishing Limited
Office 2, 3 Edgar Buildings
George Street, Bath
BA1 2FJ, UK
www.crombiejardine.com
www.twitter.com/crombiejardine

First published in 2009 by Crombie Jardine Publishing Limited

ISBN 978-1-906051-31-0

Typesetting and cover design by Ben Ottridge

Printed and bound in the UK

With thanks to Donald and Muriel

CONTENTS

INTRODUCTION...5

CHAPTER 1:
THE DIFFERENCE BETWEEN MEN AND WOMEN....................9

CHAPTER 2:
UNDERSTANDING MEN..53

CHAPTER 3:
UNDERSTANDING WOMEN..89

CHAPTER 4:
ACCEPTING THE DIFFERENCE.......................................147

INTRODUCTION

"A man falls in love through his eyes, a woman through her ears"
Woodrow Wyatt

"Find the person who will love you because of your differences and not in spite of them and you have found a lover for life"
Leo Buscaglia

"Men are from Earth. Women are from Earth. Deal with it"
George Carlin

"Nobody will ever win the battle of the sexes. There's too much fraternizing with the enemy"
Henry Kissinger

There are always exceptions to the rule but here, for the sake of ease and light-heartedness, we are going to put men into a general category and women into another…

Men fart because they can and because they find it funny. They'll play farting tunes and have contests for the loudest, smelliest or most lethal silent killers. Most women consider it rude manners, so abstain in public and let rip quietly in private. So, it could be argued that to fart or not to fart boils down to a question of pride or manners – but in general men don't give a stuff about doing it in public and women do.

Women pick flowers because flowers smell lovely, look beautiful, and offer a sense of calm. Flowers given are a symbol of love, affection, romance, apology... Unless flowers have been bought as a gesture of 'sorry', most men don't see the point of picking or buying them, only to plonk them in a vase of water and watch them slowly die over the next few days. And although it's widely known that red roses are for romance, love and passion, most men certainly wouldn't be aware that many other flowers have symbolic meanings, often complex ones. For example, a Chrysanthemum can be for a good friend, or can represent cheerfulness, or rest. A white Chrysanthemum is for truth, whilst a yellow one is for slighted love, and so forth.

Why is it that girls are seemingly born into pink, loving flowers and pretty things and boys come out ready to tumble and play fight and be joyfully fascinated with bodily functions?

Why do women adore shopping, talking, romance and being in love whilst men enjoy the lustful chase then are content to sit back with feet up, relax, watch TV, drink beer and lead a quiet life?

Or are these stereotypes just the opposite sex's way of pigeon-holing people, based on disappointing experiences, handed down to the next generation? Are some relationships doomed to go down the "s/he doesn't understand me" route? Why can't we understand the opposite sex and just appreciate them for what they are?

CHAPTER I:
The difference between men and women

APPARENT DIFFERENCES

If we look at the apparent differences between men and women today we'll probably find the following statements are generally accepted to be true:

- Women will dress up to get the paper.
  Men will shuffle down the road, having just rolled out of bed.

- Women spend ages in the bathroom, pampering themselves.
  Men leave puddles and piddles and towels on the floor, saving their toenail clipping routine for when they're lying in bed.

- Women want to be wined and dined by candlelight and soft music.
  Men want to get the spag bol down before the footie starts...

Generally, football is considered a man's territory and men don't like it being interrupted by women's chatter or, worse, by commentary in an official capacity, on the box. Look at the hoo-ha caused when Jacqui Oatley become the first female football commentator for *Match of the Day*. Football fans will no doubt side with Bill Shankly's sentiments that, "Some people think football is a matter of life and death. I don't like that attitude. I can assure them it is much more serious than that." However, many women are more likely to empathize with Erma Bombeck's, "Anybody who watched three games of football in a row should be declared brain dead."

In order to highlight the differences between what men and women want, here are two poems:

A Woman's Poem

Before I lay me down to sleep
I pray for a man who's not a creep

One who's handsome, smart and strong
One who knows his right from wrong
One who thinks before he speaks
One who'll call, not wait for weeks
I pray he's well and gainfully employed
So when I spend his cash, he's not annoyed
Someone who happily opens my doors
Massages my back and begs to do more
Oh! send me a man who'll make love to my mind
Who knows how to answer "How big is my behind?"
I pray that this man will love me no end
And be my companion, my very best friend

A Man's Poem

I pray for a mute nymphomaniac with huge boobs
who owns an off licence and a golf course
This doesn't rhyme and I don't give a shit

BATHROOM MATTERS

Another obvious area of difference between men and women is bathroom behaviour. The time spent in the bathroom can be a constant source of arguments, particularly if the toilet is in there! Even when they're not putting on make-up, why do women spend so long in there when men can be in and out in minutes?! It's all in the detail...

How to Shower Like a Woman

Take off your clothes and place them in the laundry basket according to lights and darks.

Walk to the bathroom wearing a long dressing gown.

If you see your partner, cover up any exposed areas.

Look at your womanly physique in the mirror and make a mental note to exercise more.

Get into the shower.

Use face cloth, leg cloth, long loofah, wide loofah and pumice stone.

Wash your hair once with cucumber and sage shampoo with 43 added vitamins.

Wash your hair again to make sure it is clean.

Treat your hair with grapefruit and mint enhanced conditioner.

Wash your face with crushed apricot facial scrub for 10 minutes until red.

Wash the rest of your body with ginger nut and jaffa cake body wash.

Rinse off the conditioner.

Shave your armpits and legs.

Turn off the shower.

Squeegee off all wet surfaces in the shower.

Spray mould spots with tile cleaner.

Get out of the shower.

Dry yourself with a towel the size of a small country.

Wrap your hair in a super absorbent towel.

Return to the bedroom wearing the long dressing gown.

If you see your partner, cover up any exposed areas.

How to Shower Like a Man

Take off your clothes whilst sitting on the edge of the bed and leave them in a pile on the floor.

Walk naked to the bathroom.

If you see your partner, shake your willy at her, make a face and laugh.

Marvel at your manly physique in the mirror.

Admire the size of your willy and scratch your bum.

Get in the shower.

Piss.

Wash your face.

Wash your armpits.

Blow your nose in your hands and let the water rinse it off.

Fart and laugh at how loud it sounds in the shower.

Spend the majority of the time washing your privates and the surrounding area.

Wash your bum, by sticking the bar of soap up your bum hole, leaving hairs stuck on the soap.

Wash your hair.

Make a Shampoo Mohawk.

Piss.

Rinse off shampoo and soap and get out of the shower.

Partially dry off.

Fail to notice the pool of water on the floor.

Admire your willy size in the mirror again.

Leave the wet mat on the floor and leave the light on.

If you pass your partner, pull off the towel, and shake your dick at her.

Throw the wet towel on the bed.

LANGUAGE

"A man who will not lie to a woman has very little consideration for her feelings"
Olin Miller

"I think men talk to women so they can sleep with them and women sleep with men so they can talk to them"
Jay McInerney

"I don't like compliments, and I don't see why a man should think he is pleasing a woman enormously when he says to her a whole heap of things that he doesn't mean"
Oscar Wilde

"Speak when you are angry and you will make the last speech you ever regret"
Ambrose Bierce

"I understand a fury in your words,
But not the words"
William Shakespeare

Of course conversation or, more to the point, *understanding* is important if women are to learn what men are about and vice versa. However, although we obviously speak the same language, our interpretation skills have seemingly developed at different rates…

Women are known to go around the houses to avoid being blunt, rude or spelling out something delicate that might offend. Sometimes sarcasm is a useful tool but it can be so subtle as to be undetectable to a man's ears and he will then be totally and utterly flummoxed when the full force of her anger or resentment bubbles over and ends in shouts and tears and accusations of neglect (AKA the three Ts: tantrums, tiaras and tears).

Women's English

Yes	=	No
No	=	Yes
Maybe	=	No
We need	=	I want
I am sorry	=	You'll be sorry
We need to talk	=	You're in trouble
Sure, go ahead	=	You'd better not
Do what you want	=	You will pay for this later
I am not upset	=	Of course I am upset, cretin!
You're very attentive	=	Is sex all you ever think about?

Men tend to be much less subtle and a lot more to the point, except when answering the inevitable female question passed down through the ages, "Does this make me look fat?" Innately, most men have learnt to answer this untruthfully without pausing, laughing or blinking too many times.

Men's English

I am hungry	=	I am hungry
I am sleepy	=	I am sleepy
I am tired	=	I am tired
Nice dress	=	Nice cleavage!
I love you	=	Let's have sex now
I am bored	=	Do you want to have sex?
May I have this dance?	=	I'd like to have sex with you
Can I call you sometime?	=	I'd like to have sex with you
Do you want see a film?	=	I'd like to have sex with you
Can I take you to dinner?	=	I'd like to have sex with you
Those shoes don't go	=	I'm gay

STEREOTYPES

There are those stereotypical things around the house that have become accepted as jobs for the men and jobs for the women. Why is this so? Have women just hijacked the things they like to do – i.e. the pretty, fragrant, tidying up, picking flowers and correspondence duties – whilst men like proving their strength and manliness with real men tasks such as DIY and mowing the lawn?

If men and women had the chance to send each other on training courses, what would they come up with? Perhaps something like this…

Training Courses for Men (organized by women)

Note: due to the complexity and level of difficulty of their contents, each course will accept a maximum of eight participants.

1. The After-dinner Dishes, Glasses and Cutlery:
   Can They Levitate and Fly into the Kitchen Sink?
   Examples on DVD

2. Differences Between the Laundry Basket and the Floor
   Pictures and explanatory graphics

3. Health Watch:
   Bringing Her Flowers is Not Harmful to Your Health
   Graphics and CD

4. How to Become the Ideal Shopping Companion
   Relaxation exercises, meditation and breathing techniques

5. How to Fill Ice-Cube Trays
   Step by step guide with slide presentation

6.   How to Fight Cerebral Atrophy:
     Remembering Important Dates
     Cerebral shock therapy sessions and full lobotomies offered

7.   Is it Genetically Impossible to Sit Quietly as She Parallel Parks?
     Driving simulation

8.   Learning How to Find Things:
     Starting with Looking in the Right Place Instead of Turning the
     House Upside Down While Shouting
     Open forum

9.   Learning to Live: Basic Differences Between Mother and Wife
     Online class and role-playing

10. Loss of Identity:
     Losing the Remote to Your Significant Other
     Helpline and support groups

11. Real Men Ask for Directions When Lost
    Real-life testimonials

12. Toilet Paper Rolls:
    Do They Grow on the Holders?
    Round-table discussion

Classes for Women (thought up by men)

Women think they already know everything, but wait... training courses are now available for women on the following subjects:

1. Silence, the Final Frontier:
   Where No Woman Has Gone Before

2. The Undiscovered Side of Banking:
   Making Deposits

3. Parties:
   Going Without New Outfits

4. Man Management:
   Minor Household Chores Can Wait Till After the Match

5. Bathroom Etiquette I:
   Men Need Some Space in the Bathroom Cabinet, too

6. Bathroom Etiquette II:
   His Razor Means Just That – It's His

7. Communication Skills I:
   Tears – The Last Resort, Not the First

8. Communication Skills II:
   Thinking Before Speaking

9. Communication Skills III:
   Getting What You Want Without Nagging

10. Driving a Car Safely:
    A Skill You Can Acquire

11. Telephone Skills:
    How to Hang Up

12. Introduction to Parking
    Hahahahahahaha

13. Advanced Parking:
    Backing Into a Space

14. Water Retention:
    Fact or Fat?

15. Cooking I:

    Bringing Back Bacon, Eggs and Butter

16. Cooking II:

    Bran and Tofu Are Not For Human Consumption

17. Cooking III:

    How Not to Inflict Your Diets on Other People

18. Compliments:

    Accepting Them Gracefully

19. PMS:

    Your Problem, Not His

20. Dancing:

    Why Men Don't Want To

21. Classic Footwear:
    Wearing Shoes You Already Have

22. Household Dust:
    A Harmless Natural Occurrence Only Women Notice

23. Integrating Your Laundry:
    Washing It All Together

24. Oil and Petrol:
    Your Car Needs Both

25. TV Remotes:
    For Men Only

SETTLING DOWN

"Temptation is a woman's weapon and a man's excuse"
Henry Louis Mencken

"It is better to offer no excuse than a bad one"
George Washington

"He who excuses himself accuses himself"
Gabriel Meurier

You've been on a couple of dates and you know things are not going to work out when the excuses start coming... Sometimes people just can't be upfront, either because they're cowards or because they don't want to hurt the other person, and instead of saying, "Look, it's not going to work", they offer lame excuses in the hope that you'll get the hint... These include "I'm allergic to your cat", "I'm married", "I think I'm gay" and "I'm really looking for someone to cook, clean, and iron my shirts".

Often it's at the mention of 'marriage' or 'settling down' that men get the jitters… and it has often been said that a woman marries a man expecting he will change, but he doesn't, whilst a man marries a woman expecting that she won't change and she does. Or that a woman worries about the future until she gets a husband, whilst a man never worries about the future until he gets a wife.

Of course when men and women start living together and/or get married, more than just the superficial differences between the sexes really come into play. With younger couples especially, the new wife will start off eager to please her husband and will actively take on household duties such as ironing, cooking, cleaning, washing, tidying, etc. Her underwear will be from Victoria's Secret and La Senza. This may continue for some months, even years. Usually the arrival of a baby will change the dynamics of the whole set-up and the man will suddenly find that he is (and apparently always has been) a lazy, fat, good-for-nothing slob with a one-track mind. This is when the granny knickers will make an appearance and the sparring contests kick off big time.

Here, men, are some tips for a happy marriage/living together:

✔ Buy her flowers
✔ Take her shopping
✔ Offer to cook occasionally
✔ Never forget an anniversary
✔ Buy her an eternity ring (after one year these days)
✔ Buy her a maternity ring for each child she bears
✔ Learn to change a nappy
✔ Don't mention her stretch marks – ever
✔ Don't eye up other women in front of your wife/girlfriend
✔ As far as most wives are concerned, mistresses are out of fashion

At the end of the day, the easiest thing for any married man or live-in partner is to forget his mistakes, as there is no use in two people remembering the same thing.

Husband Wanted

A lady inserted an ad in the classifieds:
"Husband Wanted"
The next day she received a hundred letters.
They all said the same thing:
"You can have mine."

With fewer and fewer couples tying the knot these days, it's hardly surprising that in a recent survey women's views on marriage were summed up as follows:

"When a woman steals your husband, there is no better revenge than to let her keep him"
Myra Venge, Bradford-on-Avon

"A woman is incomplete until she is married. Then she is finished"
Helen Earth, Bristol

"Marriage is the triumph of imagination over intelligence"
Q. Pidd, Margate

And some results from a similar survey conducted on men came up with the following takes of marriage:

"I agree with George Jean Nathan when he said that 'Marriage is based on the theory that when man discovers a brand of beer exactly to his taste he should at once throw up his job and go work in the brewery'"
Greg Garious, London

"I married Miss Right. I just didn't know her first name was Always"
Willy Makeit, Glasgow

"Married men live longer than single men. However, I've found that married men are a lot more willing to die"
Owen Cash, Dublin

"If you want your spouse to listen and pay strict attention to every word you say… talk in your sleep"
Upton O. Goode, Oxford

"Just think, if it weren't for marriage, men would go through life thinking they had no faults at all"
Seymour Clearly, London

"You have two choices in life: You can stay single and be miserable, or get married and wish you were dead"
Frank O. Pinion, Bathford

"My little boy asked me the other day, 'Daddy, how much does it cost to get married?' and I told him straight up: 'I don't know son, I'm still paying!'"
Howard I. Know, York

No Thank You, Darling

Giles asks his wife, Jules, what she would like to celebrate their wedding anniversary.

"Would you like a new fur coat?" he asks.

"Not terribly, darling," says Jules.

"Well how about a new sports car?" says Giles.

"No, not that either," she responds.

"What about a new pad in the country?" he suggests.

"No thank you, darling," says Jules.

"Well what would you like for our anniversary?" Giles asks.

"Giles, above all, I'd like a divorce," she replies.

"Eh, sorry, darling," says Giles. "You see, I wasn't planning on spending that much."

Creation

A man turned to his wife one day, exasperated, and said, "I don't know how you can be so stupid and so beautiful all at the same time!" The wife sighed and responded, "Allow me to explain. God made me beautiful so you would be attracted to me; God made me stupid so I would be attracted to you!"

Who Does What

A man and his wife were having an argument about who should brew the coffee each morning. The wife said, "You should do it, because you get up first, and then we don't have to wait as long to get our coffee." The husband said, "You are in charge of cooking around here and you should do it, because that is your job, and I can just wait for my coffee." But the wife replied, "No, you should do it, and besides, it is in the Bible that the man should do the coffee." The husband snorted and said, "I can't believe that, show me." So she fetched the Bible, and opened the New Testament and showed him at the top of several pages that it indeed says..."HEBREWS".

The Silent Treatment

A man and his wife were having some problems at home and were giving each other the silent treatment. Suddenly, the man realized that the next day he would need his wife to wake him at 5:00 a.m. for an early morning business flight. Not wanting to be the first to break the silence (and *lose*), he wrote on a piece of paper, "Please wake me at 5:00 a.m." He left it where he knew she would find it.

The next morning, the man woke up, only to discover it was 9:00 a.m. and he had missed his flight. Furious, he was about to go and see why his wife hadn't woken him, when he noticed a piece of paper by the bed. The paper said, "It is 5:00 a.m. Wake up." Men are not equipped for these kinds of contests.

You Pig!

A couple drove down a country road for several miles, not saying a word. An earlier discussion had led to an argument and neither of them wanted to concede their position. As they passed a farm full of cows, goats, and pigs, the husband asked sarcastically, "Relatives of yours?" "Yes," the wife replied, "in-laws."

Wishful Thinking

A woman was out golfing one day when she hit her ball into the woods. She went to look for it and found a frog in a trap. The frog said to her, "If you release me from this trap, I will grant you three wishes." The woman freed the frog who said, "Thank you, but I failed to mention that there was a condition to your wishes. Whatever you wish for, your husband will get… times ten!" The woman said, "That's okay."

For her first wish, she wanted to be the most beautiful woman in the world. The frog warned her, "You do realize that this wish will also make your husband the most handsome man that ever lived, an Adonis whom women will swoon over and flock to." The woman replied, "That's okay, because I will be the most beautiful woman and he will have eyes only for me." So, dada! She became the most beautiful woman in the world!

For her second wish, she wanted to be the richest woman in the world. The frog said, "That will make your husband the richest man in the world by far. And he will be ten times richer than you." The woman said, "That's okay, because what's mine is his and what's his is mine." So, dada! She became the richest woman in the world.

The frog then inquired about her third wish and, after careful consideration, she answered, "I'd like a mild heart attack."

Moral of the story:
Women are clever. Don't mess with them.

Attention!
Female readers: This is the end of the joke for you. Stop here and continue feeling good.
Male readers: Please continue...

The man had a heart attack ten times milder than his wife!!!

Moral of the story:
Women are really dumb but think they're really smart. Let them continue to think that way and just enjoy the show.

P.S.: If you are a woman and still reading this, it only goes to show that women are nosey and never listen!

Computer Man

Let's look at the female / male approach to the same scene.

A Spanish teacher was explaining to her class that in Spanish, unlike English, nouns are designated as either masculine or feminine. 'House' for instance, is feminine ('la casa'), whilst 'pencil' is masculine ('el lapiz').

A student asked, "What gender is 'computer'?" Instead of giving the answer, the teacher split the class into two groups, male and female, and asked them to decide for themselves whether 'computer' should be a masculine or a feminine noun. Each group was asked to give four reasons for its recommendation.

The men's group decided that 'computer' should definitely be of the feminine gender ('la computadora'), because:

1. No-one but their creator understands their internal logic.

2. The native language they use to communicate with other computers is incomprehensible to everyone else.

3. Even the smallest mistakes are stored in long term memory for possible later retrieval.

4. As soon as you make a commitment to one, you find yourself spending half your salary on accessories for it.

The women's group, however, concluded that computers should be masculine ('el computador'), because:

1. In order to do anything with them, you have to turn them on.

2. They have a lot of data but still can't think for themselves.

3. They are supposed to help you solve problems, but half the time they *are* the problem.

4. As soon as you commit to one, you realize that if you had waited a little longer, you could have got a better model.

The women won.

"The trouble with her is that she lacks the power of conversation, but not the power of speech"
George Bernard Shaw

"Men are superior to women. For one thing, they can urinate from a speeding car"
Will Durst

Husbandstore

A husband shop (Husbandstore) has just opened where a woman can go to choose a husband from among many contenders. The shop comprises six floors, and the men increase in positive attributes as the shopper ascends the flights. There is, however, a catch… As you open the door to any floor you may choose a man from that floor, but if you go up a floor, you cannot go back down except to leave the building and not return. Once you have left, you will not remember anything about the experience.

So a woman goes to the shop to find a husband…

On the first floor the sign on the door reads: "Floor 1: These men have jobs." The woman reads the sign and says to herself, "Well, that's better than my last boyfriend, but I wonder what's further up?" So up she goes.

The second floor sign reads: "Floor 2: These men have jobs and love kids." The woman remarks to herself, "That's great, but I wonder what's further up?" And up she goes again.

The third floor sign reads: "Floor 3: These men have jobs, love kids and are extremely good looking." "Hmmm, better," she says, "but I wonder what's upstairs?"

The fourth floor sign reads: "Floor 4: These men have jobs, love kids, are extremely good looking and help with the housework." "Wow!" exclaims the woman, "very tempting... but there must be more further up!" And again she heads up another flight.

The fifth floor sign reads: "Floor 5: These men have jobs, love kids, are extremely good looking, help with the housework and have a strong romantic streak." "Oh, mercy me," she says, "but just think what must be on the next level?!" So up to the sixth floor she goes.

The sixth floor sign reads:"Floor 6:You are visitor 123,456,789,012 to this floor. There are no men on this floor. This floor exists solely as proof that women are impossible to please. Thank you for shopping at Husbandstore. Have a nice day."

A Taxing Job

A young man married a beautiful woman who had previously divorced ten husbands. On their wedding night she told her new husband, "Please be gentle, I'm still a virgin." "What?!" said the puzzled groom, "How's that possible if you've been married ten times before?"

"Well, husband no. 1 was a Sales Representative. He kept telling me how great it was going to be.
"Husband no. 2 was in Software Support. He was never really sure how it was supposed to function, but he said he'd look into it and get back to me.

"Husband no. 3 was from Field Services. He said everything checked out diagnostically but he just couldn't get the system up.

"Husband no. 4 was in Telemarketing. Even though he knew he had the order, he didn't know when he would be able to deliver.

"Husband no. 5 was an engineer. He understood the basic process but wanted three years to research, implement and design a new state-of-the-art method.

"Husband no. 6 was from Finance and Administration. He thought he knew how, but he wasn't sure whether it was his job or not.

"Husband no. 7 was in Marketing. Although he had a product, he was never sure how to position it.

"Husband no. 8 was a psychiatrist. All he ever did was talk about it.

"Husband no. 9 was a gynaecologist. All he did was look at it.

"Husband no. 10 was a stamp collector. All he ever did was... God! I do miss him! But now that I've married you, I'm so excited!"

"Glad to hear it!" said the husband, "But why?"

"With a taxman I know I'm gonna get screwed!"

You're Right, I'm Wrong

A husband and wife were involved in a petty argument, both of them unwilling to admit they might be in error. "I'll admit I'm wrong," the wife told her husband in a conciliatory attempt, "if you'll admit I'm right." He agreed and, like a gentleman, he insisted she go first. "OK, I'm wrong," she said. With a twinkle in his eye, he responded, "You're right!"

Tesco Husband

Proof of what can happen if a wife or girlfriend drags her husband or boyfriend along shopping is best highlighted by a letter apparently once sent by Tesco's Head Office to a customer in Oxford. After thanking Mrs Murray for her valued custom and the use of her Tesco Loyalty Card, the letter went on to explain that unfortunately the Manager of the Tesco's store in Banbury was considering banning

Mrs Murray and family from shopping with Tesco, unless her husband stopped "his antics".

Here is a list of Mr Murray's alleged offences during the six month period prior to the letter – all offences had been "verified by our surveillance cameras":

1. June 15: Took 24 boxes of condoms and randomly put them in people's trolleys when they weren't looking.

2. July 2: Set all the alarm clocks in Housewares to go off at 5-minute intervals.

3. July 7: Made a trail of tomato juice on the floor leading to the Feminine Products aisle.

4. July 19: Walked up to an employee and told her in an official tone, "Code 3 in Housewares"... and watched what happened.

5. August 14: Moved a 'CAUTION – WET FLOOR' sign to a carpeted area.

6. September 15: Set up a tent in the Outdoor Clothing department and told shoppers he'd invite them in if they would bring sausages and a Calor gas stove.

7. September 23: When the Deputy Manager asked if she could help him, he began to cry and asked, "Why can't you people just leave me alone?"

8. November 10: While appearing to be choosing kitchen knives in the Housewares aisle he asked an assistant if he knew where the antidepressants were.

9. December 3: Darted around the store suspiciously, loudly humming the 'Mission Impossible' theme.

10. December 6: In the Kitchenware aisle, practised the 'Madonna look' using different size funnels.

11. December 18: Hid in a clothing rack and when people browsed, yelled "PICK ME! PICK ME!"

12. December 21: When an announcement came over the loudspeaker, assumed the foetal position and screamed "NO! NO! It's those voices again."

And last, but not least:

13. December 23: Went into a fitting room, shut the door, waited a while; then yelled, very loudly, "There is no toilet paper in here!"

[Men v. Shopping. Case closed, m'lud.]

CHAPTER 2:
Understanding Men

BOYS WILL BE BOYS

"Boys will be boys, and so will a lot of middle-aged men"
Kin Hubbard

"Progress isn't made by early risers. It's made by lazy men trying to find easier ways to do something"
Robert Heinlein

"The only time a woman really succeeds in changing a man is when he's a baby"
Natalie Wood

FACTOID

Did you know..?
Most men have erections every 60 to 90 minutes during sleep.

Because I'm a Man... Ten Basic Steps To Understanding Men

1: Because I'm a man, when I lock my keys in the car, I will fiddle with a coat hanger long after hypothermia has set in. Calling the AA is not an option. I will win.

2: Because I'm a man, when the car isn't running very well, I will lift the bonnet and stare at the engine as if I know what I'm looking at. If another man shows up, one of us will say to the other, "I used to be able to fix these things, but now with all these computers and everything, I wouldn't know where to start." We will then drink a couple of beers and break wind, as a form of holy communion.

3: Because I'm a man, when I catch a cold, I need someone to bring me soup and take care of me while I lie in bed and moan. You're a woman. You never get as sick as I do, so for you, this is no problem.

4: Because I'm a man, I can be relied upon to purchase basic groceries at the supermarket, like milk or bread. I cannot be expected to find exotic items like 'cumin' or 'tofu'. For all I know, these are the same thing.

5: Because I'm a man, when one of our appliances stops working, I will insist on taking it apart, despite evidence that this will just cost me twice as much once the repair person gets here and has to put it back together.

6: Because I'm a man, I must hold the television remote control in my hand while I watch TV. If the thing has been misplaced, I may miss a whole show looking for it, blaming others living in the house, and yelling because they are not desperately searching for it with the urgency it requires.

7: Because I'm a man, there is no need to ask me what I'm thinking about. The true answer is always sex, cars or sport. I have to make up something else when you ask, so just don't ask.

8: Because I'm a man, you don't have to ask me if I liked the film. Chances are, if you're crying at the end of it, I didn't... and if you are feeling amorous afterwards then I will certainly remember the name of it and recommend it to others.

9: Because I'm a man, I think what you're wearing is fine. I thought what you were wearing five minutes ago was fine too. Either pair of shoes is fine... with the belt or without it, looks fine. It does not make your arse look too big. That was the chocolate, pizzas and alcohol. Your hair is fine. You look fine. Can we just go now?

10: Because I'm a man, and this is, after all, the 21st century, I will share equally in the housework. You just do the laundry, the cooking, the cleaning, the vacuuming, and the dishes, and I'll do the rest. Like wandering around in the garden with a beer, wondering what to do.

Men like an easy life. "What's wrong with that?" they'll cry. That's not to say they can't be bothered to get off their backsides. Look at all the powerful men holding top positions in companies throughout the world. But it has to be said that there is a certain outlook amongst the general male population in this country and others that if there are two ways of doing something, it makes no sense to opt for the most difficult option and that sometimes wonderful opportunities come from doing things the alternative or non-conformist way. Then you can get back to doing what you like best. But it does mean that men will conveniently learn not to be bothered about mess and dirt and untidiness and cooking – basically the things that women *are* bothered about – safe in the knowledge (or wishful thinking) that if they ignore it, it will, in all likelihood and with a bit of luck, go away.

A typical 'man-bashing' joke for women will go along the lines of this:

Men are like…

…laxatives: they irritate the shit out of you
…bananas: the older they get, the less firm they are
…holidays: they never seem to be long enough
…weather: nothing can be done to change them
…coffee: the best are rich, hot, and can keep you up all night
…government bonds: they take soooooooo long to mature
…mascara: they usually run at the first sign of emotion
…popcorn: they satisfy you, but only for a little while

This gives a small amount of insight into what women like and dislike about men, what they look for in a partner, etc. General topics that women can find infuriating or just hard to understand can range from why men have a problem with putting the toilet seat down and why men won't ask for directions to why do men find it so difficult to express their feelings?

The Guys' Rules

A lot is said about how women like to make rules, that they insist on things being just so and how they expect men to know all their written and unwritten rules by instinct and training. Well, guys across the country are fed up with this and at last a man has taken the time to write The Guys' Rules*. So here we have 'The Rules' from the male perspective:

(* *Females please note*: these rules are all numbered "1" *on purpose*!)

1. Men are *not* mind readers.

1. Learn to work the toilet seat. You're a big girl. If it's up, put it down. We need it up, you need it down. You don't hear us complaining about you leaving it down, do you?

1. Sunday sports. It's like the full moon or the changing of the tides. Let it be.

1. Shopping is *not* a sport and we are never going to think of it that way.

1. Crying is blackmail.

1. Ask for what you want. Let us be clear on this one: Subtle hints do not work! Strong hints do not work! Obvious hints do not work! Just say it!

1. 'Yes' and 'No' are perfectly acceptable answers to almost every question.

1. Come to us with a problem only if you want help solving it. That's what we do. Sympathy is what your girlfriends are for.

1. A headache that lasts for 17 months is a problem. See a doctor.

1. Anything we said six months ago is inadmissible in an argument. In fact, all comments become null and void after seven days. If you won't dress like the Victoria's Secret girls, don't expect us to act like soap opera guys.

1. If you think you're fat, you probably are. Don't ask us.

1. If something we said can be interpreted in two ways and one of the ways makes you sad or angry, we meant the other one.

1. You can either ask us to do something *or* tell us how you want it done. Not both. If you already know best how to do it, just do it yourself.

1. Whenever possible, please say whatever you have to say during the advert breaks.

1. Christopher Columbus did not need to ask for directions and neither do we.

1. *All* men see in only 16 colours, like Windows default settings. Peach, for example, is a fruit, not a colour. Pumpkin is also a fruit. We have no idea what 'mauve' is.

1. If it itches, it will be scratched. We do that.

1. If we ask what is wrong and you say "nothing", we will act like nothing's wrong. We know you are lying, but it is just not worth the hassle.

1. If you ask a question you don't want an answer to, expect an answer you don't want to hear.

1. When we have to go somewhere, absolutely anything you wear is fine... really.

1. Don't ask us what we're thinking about unless you are prepared to discuss such topics as sex, cars and sport.

1. You have enough clothes.

1. You have too many shoes.

1. I am in shape. Round *is* a shape!

1. Thank you for reading this. Yes, I know, I have to sleep on the sofa tonight; but did you know that men really don't mind that? It's like camping.

Things a Man Likes About a Woman

- She listens to him
- She approves of his job
- She approves of his mum
- She doesn't expect him to eat with her parents every Sunday
- She likes the presents he buys
- She's independent
- She admits to loving sex (especially with him)
- She lets him hang out with his mates
- She freely lets him watch sport whenever he wants
- She happily lets him drink beer
- She doesn't tell him he's driving too fast/aggressively/he's lost
- She can read maps
- She doesn't feel threatened by his ex-girlfriends
- SHE DOESN'T NAG HIM
- She has a rich dad

IMPULSES AND SEX

Things a Woman Should Know About the Average Guy

Average length of penis when not erect: 3.5 inches

Average length when erect: 5 inches

Average number of times a man will ejaculate in his lifetime: 7,200

Average number of sperm in an ejaculation: 300 million

Average number of spurts in one ejaculation: 5

Average number of erections per day: 11

Average number of erections during the night: 9

Average number of men who come before they want to: 25%

Obviously men's actions are driven by a variety of urges but some are more overwhelming than others. Acting on visual impulses is a strong male feature…

The Blonde in the Casino

An attractive blonde from Dublin arrived in the casino and bet £20,000 on a single roll of the dice.

She said, "I hope you don't mind, but I feel much luckier when I'm completely nude." With that, she stripped completely, rolled the dice and yelled, "Come on, baby, Mama needs new clothes!"

As the dice came to a stop, she jumped up and down, wiggled and squealed... "YES! YES! I WON, I WON!" She hugged each of the dealers and then picked up her winnings and her clothes and quickly departed.

The dealers stared at each other dumbfounded. Finally, one of them asked, "What did she roll?" The other answered, "I don't know – I thought you were watching."

Moral of the story:
Not all Irish are stupid and not all blondes are dumb, but all men are men.

Nursery Rhymes

Men like to laugh at things they found funny as boys – farting, scaring girls, etc. – so it should come as no surprise that nursery puddings like spotted dick and shaving cream are still top of men's favourite foods list and that nursery rhymes have been known to be altered to suit the more 'mature' male...

Mary had a little skirt
With splits right up the sides
And every time that Mary walked
The boys could see her thighs
Mary had another skirt
It was split right up the front
But she didn't wear that one very often

Little Miss Muffet sat on a tuffet
Her clothes all tattered and torn
It wasn't the spider that crept up beside her
But Little Boy Blue with the horn

Simple Simon met a Pieman
Going to the fair
Said Simple Simon to the Pieman
"What have you got there?"
Said the Pieman to Simple Simon
"Pies, you dickhead!"

Humpty Dumpty sat on a wall
Humpty Dumpty had a great fall
All the kings horses and all the kings men
Said, "Sod him, he's only an egg."

Mary had a little lamb
It ran into a pylon
10,000 volts went up its ar–
And turned its wool to nylon

Georgie Porgy pudding and pie
Kissed the girls and made them cry
When the boys came out to play
He kissed them too as he was gay

Jack and Jill went up the hill
To have some hanky panky
Silly Jill forgot her pill
And now there's little Frankie

Humpty Dumpty sat on a wall
Humpty Dumpty had a great fall
All the kings' horses
And all the kings' men
Had scrambled eggs
For breakfast again

There was a little girl who had a little curl
Right in the middle of her forehead
When she was good, she was very, very good
But when she was bad...
She got jewellery, a waterfront apartment, and a sports car

Obsessed with sex? Men will argue that they just have a healthy no-nonsense approach to their body. They don't have hang-ups about not being tanned, having a few wrinkles or grey hairs. OK, penis envy *is* an issue, but generally speaking men are proud of what they've got.

The Day the Penis asked for a Raise

I, the Penis, hereby request a raise in salary for the following reasons:

- I do physical labour
- I work at great depths
- I plunge headfirst into everything I do
- I do not get weekends or public holidays off
- I work in a damp environment

- I work in a dark workplace that has poor ventilation
- I work in high temperatures
- My work exposes me to contagious diseases.

Sincerely,

P. Niss

The Response

Dear P. Niss,

After assessing your request, and considering the arguments you have raised, the administration rejects your request for the following reasons:

- You do not work 8 hours straight
- You fall asleep after brief work periods
- You do not always follow the orders of the management team

- You do not stay in your designated area and are often seen visiting other locations
- You do not take initiative – you need to be pressured and stimulated in order to start working
- You leave the workplace rather messy at the end of your shift
- You don't always observe necessary safety regulations, such as wearing the correct protective clothing
- You will retire well before you are 65
- You are unable to work double shifts
- You sometimes leave your designated work area before you have completed your assigned task
- And if that were not all, you have been seen constantly entering and exiting the workplace carrying two suspicious-looking bags.

Sincerely,

V. Jynah

Blown Away

Larry got home late one night and his wife, Linda, demanded, "Where do you think you've been?" Larry replied, "I was out getting a tattoo." "A tattoo?" she frowned. "What kind of tattoo did you get?" "I got a fifty quid note on my privates," he said proudly. "What the hell were you thinking?" she said, shaking her head in disdain. "Why on earth would an accountant get a £50 note tattooed on his privates?" "Well… One, I like to watch my money grow. Two, once in a while I like to play with my money. Three, I like how money feels in my hand. And lastly, instead of you going out shopping, you can stay right here at home and blow £50 anytime you want!"

"I'm such a good lover because I practise a lot on my own"
Woody Allen

"How lucky we are that we can reach our genitals instead of that spot on our back that itches?"
Flash Rosenberg

"Masturbation: the primary sexual activity of mankind. In the nineteenth century it was a disease; in the twentieth, it's a cure"
Thomas Szasz

And what is the big deal about masturbating anyway? It doesn't mean anything negative about the relationship men are in. It's a basic urge, nothing more, nothing less. As George Carlin put it so succinctly, "If God had intended us not to masturbate, He would have made our arms shorter."

A few years ago the Hite report apparently concluded that 95% of men masturbate, and 54% admit to doing so once a day. Sadly, 41% said they feel guilty about it. 70% of women said they'd masturbated.

FACTOID

Did you know..?

Every year, some 11,000 Americans injure themselves while trying out bizarre sexual positions.

A Liverpool Love Story

A young woman in Liverpool was so depressed that she decided to end her life by throwing herself into the Mersey. She went down to the docks and was about to leap into the freezing water when a handsome young sailor saw her tottering on the edge of the pier, crying.

He took pity on her and said, "Look, you have so much to live for. I'm off to America in the morning, and if you like, I can stow you away on my ship. I'll take good care of you and bring you food every day."

Moving closer, he slipped his arm round her shoulder and added, "I'll keep you happy, and you'll keep me happy." The girl nodded. After all, what did she have to lose? Perhaps a fresh start in America would give her life new meaning. That night, the sailor brought her aboard and hid her in a lifeboat.

From then on, every night he brought her three sandwiches and a piece of fruit, and they made passionate love until dawn.

Two weeks later, during a routine inspection, she was discovered by the captain. "What are you doing here?" the captain asked. "I have an arrangement with one of the sailors," she explained, "I get food and a trip to America, and he's screwing me." "He certainly is!" the captain said, "This is the Birkenhead Ferry."

The Big Test

Englishmen might be a little more reserved than other men but probably no less insensitive to the needs of women. Here's the story of a gentleman who'd rather not be named:

I was a very happy person. My wonderful girlfriend and I had been dating for over a year, and so we decided to get married. There was only one little thing bothering me... It was her beautiful younger sister.

My prospective sister-in-law was twenty-two, wore very tight mini-skirts, and generally went braless. She would regularly bend down when she was near me, and I always got more than a pleasant view of her private parts. It had to be deliberate; she never did it when she was near anyone else.

One day my girlfriend's 'little' sister called and asked me to come over to check the wedding invitations. She was alone when I arrived and she whispered to me that she had feelings and desires for me that she couldn't overcome.

She told me that she wanted to make love to me just once before I got married and committed my life to her sister.

Well, I was in total shock, and couldn't say a word. She said, "I'm going upstairs to my bedroom, and if you want one last wild fling, just come up and get me."

I was stunned and frozen in shock as I watched her go up the stairs. When she reached the top she pulled off her panties and threw them down the stairs at me. I stood there for a moment, then turned and made a beeline for the front door. I opened the door, and headed for my car.

Lo and behold, my entire future family was standing outside, all clapping! With tears in his eyes, my father-in-law hugged me and said, "We are very happy that you have passed our little test. We couldn't ask for a better man for our eldest daughter. Welcome to the family!"

And the moral of this story:
Always keep your condoms in your car.

FARTING

Farting is technically a sport for men and sport is a big part of men's lives, whether it's the high-powered cliqueiness of top golf clubs, cricket on the village green, tennis on the TV, or football at home and away. Actually playing sports brings out those competitive boys whose aim is still to win and be the best. After all, if winning isn't important, why bother to keep score? Those good at sports will go at it hammer and tong; those less well blessed athletically may take Alfred Hitchcock's view that, "There's nothing to winning, really. That is, if you happen to be blessed with a keen eye, an agile mind and no scruples whatsoever"…

Watching sport gets the men together, drinking beer, scoffing pizza, farting and having fun. Women should not try to break into this routine any more than men should try to join a girlie bonding shopping trip into the West End followed by a few bottles of Chardonnay in a charming little wine bar.

FACTOID

Did you know..?

The average person releases nearly a pint of intestinal gas in the form of farting every day. This is equivalent to about fourteen farts. Most of this is due to swallowed air. The rest is from fermentation of undigested food.

The joy of farting. It's just funny, that's all… Who, as a schoolboy, didn't at some stage hear that farts burn because they contain the highly flammable gases methane and hydrogen? How many schoolboys have tried to light their fights as a result? Many men will be able to tell you that farts tend to burn with a blue or yellow flame. Not a lot of women know (or have seen) that! And as for the schoolboys' hero, Monsieur Le Petomane… what a star! To earn a living from farting performances..!

The appeal of farts has even spread to eBay, where it has been known for a fart in a jar to be put up for sale…

FACTOID

Did you know..?

A man is most likely to fart first thing in the morning, while in the toilet. Sometimes referred to as 'morning thunder', it can be heard from some distance and is often accompanied by a heartfelt, "Ahhhh! Ya bundie!"

Apparently, despite practically everyone in the world thinking to the contrary, women fart just as much as men. Men obviously just take more pride in the activity than most women. There is a big difference between individuals in the amount of farting they do but apparently any difference is definitely not down to gender – but rather diet, way of eating, etc. So why do women tend to deny farting? Because they think it's rude!

FACTOID

Did you know..?

If you hold in your farts during the day you are just storing up all that gas which will let itself out – either at night, when you sleep and your body relaxes, or at another stage when you least expect it (and it will be worse then, as it's travelled back up your system a bit and will be more anxious to get out).

"Because of their cuisine, Germans don't consider farting rude. They'd certainly be out of luck if they did."
P.J. O'Rourke

Man Joke

Why do men break wind more than women?
Because women can't shut up long enough to build up the required pressure.

What to do if You Fart Unexpectedly

- Blame it on your squeaky shoes.
- Turn to the person next to you and say that you heard it but they shouldn't be embarrassed.
- Blame the floorboards in these old houses.

- Feign a coughing fit and hope it makes people think that they heard the wrong end.
- Kick the dog.

What to do if You Fart in a Lift

- Stand back and enjoy it.

Farting Fit for a Queen

At Heathrow, a 300-foot-long red carpet is stretched out to Air Force One and President Bush strides to a warm but dignified handshake from Queen Elizabeth II. They ride in a silver 1934 Bentley limousine to the edge of central London where they board an open 17th-century coach hitched to six magnificent white matching horses. They ride towards Buckingham Palace, each looking sideways and waving to the thousands of cheering Brits lining the streets. All is going well. Suddenly the right rear horse lets rip with the most horrendous, earth-rending, eye-smarting blast of gastronomic flatulence ever heard in the British Empire, including Bermuda, Tortola and the Falkland Islands. It shakes the coach. Uncomfortable, but in control, the two dignitaries of state do their best to pretend nothing has happened. The Queen then turns to Mr Bush and says, "Mr President, please accept my regrets. I'm sure you understand that there are some things that even a Queen cannot control." George W. Bush, ever the gentleman, replies, "Your Majesty, please don't give the matter another thought. You know, if you hadn't said something, I would have thought it was one of the horses..."

CHAPTER 3:
Understanding Women

"Men who don't understand women fall into two groups: Bachelors and Husbands"
Jacques Languirand

"The great question that has never been answered and which I have not yet been able to answer, despite my thirty years of research into the feminine soul, is, 'What does a woman want?'"
Sigmund Freud

"A gentleman always remembers a woman's birthday but never remembers her age"
Anon

"Every woman is wrong until she cries, and then she is right, instantly"
Anon

"A successful man is one who makes more money than his wife can spend"
Anon

"There are a number of mechanical devices which increase sexual arousal, particularly in women. Chief among these is the Mercedes-Benz 380SL"
Lynn Lavner

FLOWER POWER

"Arranging a bowl of flowers in the morning can give a sense of quiet in a crowded day – like writing a poem"
Anne Morrow Lindbergh

"Gardens and flowers have a way of bringing people together, drawing them from their homes"
Clare Ansberry

"Money is a powerful aphrodisiac. But flowers work almost as well"
Robert Heinlein

"If I had a single flower for every time I think about you, I could walk forever in my garden"
Claudia Ghandi

"Life is a flower of which love is the honey"
Victor Hugo

Flowers are a luxury, a gift, a token of love, an expression of friendship, gratitude, and so forth. They can cheer up a room, dress a dinner table and add the finishing touch to a wedding. They are not a necessity but a natural beauty which is why they are loved.

Part of the attraction with flowers is that they have a strong link to romance and unspoken language. Way back in medieval and

Renaissance times, flowers had moral meanings. In paintings, for example, a white rose would often symbolize chastity. In Victorian times, with such a strict moral code in place, the language of flowers was a subtle means of communication and flowers were used to send coded messages.

Most of the subtlety involved in floriography has long since been forgotten, yet still today most people would appreciate that red roses signify romance.

FACTOID

Did you know..?

Poinsettias are popular at Christmas time, often used to make the home more festive looking. The Aztecs used poinsettias in several ways, mainly as a type of medicine or as a dye. The poinsettia was named after the man who discovered it: Joel Poinsett. The red 'flowers' are, in fact, leaves.

Here are some classic meanings to flowers:

Acacia		Secret love
Campanula		Gratitude
Carnation	(pink)	A woman's love
	(red)	My heart aches
	(yellow)	Rejection
Chrysanthemum	(red)	I love you
Daffodil		Uncertainty, respect, unrequited love
Daisy		Innocence, loyal love, purity
Forget-me-not		True love
Honeysuckle		True affection
Morning glory		Love in vain
Rose	(red)	True love
	(white)	Eternal love, innocence, virtue, purity
	(yellow)	Friendship, platonic love
Tulip	(red)	Declaration of love

TIME MANAGEMENT

Women have to do everything, don't they? Pick up the pieces when their friends break up with their boyfriends, find whole outfits to buy for special occasions, manage the household, and often keep down a full-time job whilst being expected to be a perfect mother, friend, cook, cleaner, chauffeur, accountant, confidante, wife and sex goddess in the bedroom. It's no wonder they lose their rags sometimes!

The 21st-Century Version of the Three Bears

A far more accurate account of the events of that fateful morning in the woods...

Baby Bear goes downstairs, sits in his small chair at the table and he looks into his small bowl. It is empty. "Who's been eating my porridge?" he squeaks miserably.

Daddy Bear arrives at the table and sits in his big chair. He looks into his big bowl and it is also empty. "Who's been eating my porridge?!?" he roars angrily.

Mummy Bear puts her head through the serving hatch from the kitchen and yells, "For God's sake, how many times do we have to go through this with you idiots?

"It was Mummy Bear who got up first.

"It was Mummy Bear who woke up everyone in the house.

"It was Mummy Bear who made the coffee.

"It was Mummy Bear who unloaded the dishwasher from last night and put everything away.

"It was Mummy Bear who went out in the cold, wet early morning air to fetch the newspaper.

"It was Mummy Bear who set the damn table.

"It was Mummy Bear who put the bloody cats out, cleaned the litter boxes, gave the cats their food, and refilled their water. And now that you've decided to drag your sorry bear-selves downstairs and grace Mummy Bear with your grumpy presence, listen carefully because I'm only going to say this once: I HAVEN'T MADE THE EFFING PORRIDGE YET!!!"

FACTOID

Did you know..?
According to The Sun, 3 June 2009, two-thirds of women would rather start the day with a cup of tea than sex, a poll showed.

"Never have more children than you have car windows"
Erma Bombeck

THE LANGUAGE OF ROMANCE AND PMS (SO INEXTRICABLY LINKED)

Apparently, one disgruntled woman once said that a man is like a deck of cards because you need:

- *A Heart to love him*
- *A Diamond to marry him*
- *A Club to smash his stupid head in*
- *A Spade to bury the bastard*

It could have just been her time of the month or a string of bad relationships ending in a divorce... whatever. It is generally agreed that most women are after a man who'll keep them in the style they would like to become accustomed to. But first off, women want to be appreciated. So in the morning when the alarm clock goes off, they do not want to be met with snoring, farting, burping or the scratching of bollocks, but rather a kiss and the offer of a cup of tea in bed...

In this day and age marriage is probably not on many women's minds, even when they hear the deafening tick of the biological clock. But the desire for romance is certainly not dead. Things that go down well with the ladies include:

- Firelight, candles and dimmed lights. It makes them feel more comfortable about getting naked.
- Gentlemen who know how to remove knickers and brassieres with panache. Finger fumbles are a no-no.
- Getting on with her parents.
- The ability to gauge her feelings: whether it's the desire for a bodice-ripping scene or a long seduction… or just chocolate.
- Chocolate. Always appreciated. Rarely willingly shared.
- Opening doors for her – whether they be of the car, theatre, restaurant or front variety.
- Being able to locate the G-spot (not that you'd ask for directions).

- Complimenting her on her appearance (but don't get too specific).
- Listening to her. Properly.
- Saying how much you enjoy her cooking (even if you are normally desperate to give it to the cat).
- Calling, like you said you would.
- Flowers. Never underestimate flower power.

FACTOID

Did you know..?

The average sexual experience last about 40 minutes.

Adonis in Flight

On a transatlantic flight, a plane passes through a severe storm. The turbulence is awful, and things go from bad to worse when one wing is struck by lightning.

One woman in particular loses it and starts screaming, "I'm too young to die!" Then she yells, "Well, if I'm going to die, I want my last minutes to be memorable! Is there anyone on this plane who can make me feel like a woman?"

For a moment there is silence. Everyone stares at the desperate woman at the front of the plane. Then an Italian man stands up at the rear of the plane. He is gorgeous: tall, well built, with dark brown hair and eyes. He starts to walk slowly up the aisle, unbuttoning his shirt, one button at a time. No one moves. He removes his shirt. Muscles ripple across his chest. The woman gasps. He whispers: "Iron this, and get me something to eat."

FACTOID
Did you know..?
The average couple spends 14 minutes on foreplay.

A Woman's Prayer

Dear Lord, I pray for wisdom
to understand a man
to love and to forgive him
and for patience, for his moods
because, Lord, if I pray for strength
I'll just beat him to death

"Intimate relationships cannot substitute for a life plan. But to have any meaning or viability at all, a life plan must include intimate relationships"
Harriet Lerner

FACTOID

Did you know..?
The longest kiss in the Guinness Book of World Records lasted 417 hours!

Women tend to be romantics and often feel at a loss without a partner / boyfriend. Sometimes, they will opt for personal ads and this is where the interpretation of their language calls for some flexibility... Bear in mind that age is a sensitive issue once a women has reached 40 and weight is always an issue. Often the language is not deceitful on purpose, it's just a way of avoiding a few unpleasant home truths.

Dictionary for Women's Personal Ads

40-ish	-	49
Adventurous	-	Slept with everyone
Athletic	-	No tits
Average looking	-	Ugly
Beautiful	-	Pathological liar
Emotionally secure	-	On medication
Feminist	-	Fat

Free spirit	-	Junkie
Fun	-	Annoying
New Age	-	Body hair in the wrong places
Open-minded	-	Desperate
Outgoing	-	Loud and embarrassing
Passionate	-	Sloppy drunk
Professional	-	Bitch
Voluptuous	-	Very fat
Large frame	-	Hugely fat
Wants soulmate	-	Stalker

Hormonal Sounds and Phrases

Sometimes a woman will just be hormonally annoyed and will say something to a man that inevitably hides a darker truth but she's in no mood to humour him and he'll learn in due course how she really feels – revenge is a dish best served cold, and all that…

So keywords and noises in a woman's vocabulary will generally include:

- *"Fine"*

This is the word women use at the end of any argument in which they feel they are right, but need to shut you up. Never say "Fine" to describe how a woman looks. This will cause you to have one of those arguments.

- *"Five minutes"*

This is half an hour. It is equivalent to the five minutes that your football game is going to last before you take out the rubbish, so women feel that it's an even trade.

- *"Nothing"*

This means something and you should be on your toes. "Nothing" is commonly used to describe the feeling a woman has of wanting to turn you inside out. "Nothing" usually signifies an argument that will last "Five minutes" and end with the word "Fine".

● *"Go ahead" (with raised eyebrows)*
This is a dare. One that will result in a woman getting upset over "Nothing" and it will all end with the word "Fine".

● *"Go ahead" (normal eyebrows)*
This means "I give up" or "Do what you want because I don't care". You will get a raised eyebrow "Go ahead" in just a few minutes, followed by "Nothing" and "Fine" and she will talk to you in about "Five minutes" when she cools off.

● *"[Loud sigh]"*
This is not actually a word, but is still often a verbal statement very misunderstood by men. A "Loud sigh" means she thinks you are an idiot at that moment and wonders why she is wasting her time standing there and arguing with you over "Nothing".

- *"[Soft sigh]"*

Again, not a word, but a verbal statement. "Soft sighs" are one of the few things that some men actually understand. She is content. Your best bet is to not move or breathe and she will stay content.

- *"Oh"*

This word followed by any statement is trouble. Example: "Oh, let me get that." Or, "Oh, I talked to him about what you were doing last night." If she says "Oh" before a statement, run, do not walk, to the nearest exit. She will tell you that she is "Fine" when she is done tossing your clothes out the window, but do not expect her to talk to you for at least three days. "Oh" at the beginning of a sentence usually signifies that you are caught in a lie. Do not try to lie more to get out of it, or you will get raised eyebrows and a "Go ahead", followed by acts so unspeakable that they cannot be written about here.

● *"That's okay"*

This is one of the most dangerous statements that a woman can make to a man. "That's okay" means that she wants to think long and hard before visiting on you major retribution and tribulations for whatever it is that you have done. "That's okay" is often used with the word "Fine" and in conjunction with a raised eyebrow "Go ahead". At some point in the near future when she has plotted and planned, you are going to be in some mighty big trouble.

● *"Please do"*

This is not a statement; it is an offer. A woman is giving you the chance to come up with whatever excuse or reason you have for doing whatever it is that you have done. You have a fair chance to tell the truth, so be careful and you shouldn't get a "That's okay".

● *"Thanks"*

A woman is thanking you. Do not faint, just say "You're welcome".

- *"Thanks a lot"*

This is in no way like "Thanks". A woman will say, "Thanks a lot" when she is really ticked off at you. It signifies that you have hurt her in some callous way, and "Thanks a lot" will be followed by the "Loud sigh". Be careful not to ask what is wrong after the "Loud sigh", as she will only tell you "Nothing".

Women's sensitivity and romantic nature can sometimes obscure ruthless, some might say even pathological and psychotic, behavioural traits... These can be simply explained for the most part by hormones, especially at THAT TIME OF THE MONTH... Men should never ask if a woman has her period as this implies that she is cranky, spotty, fat and unreasonable. If she has got her period she will shout something like, "Oh yes, put it down to that, why don't you? What do you know?" And if she hasn't got her period she'll demand to know what you are insinuating. Be warned.

15 Things PMS Stands For

1. Pass My Shotgun
2. Psychotic Mood Shift
3. Perpetual Munching Spree
4. Puffy Mid-Section
5. People Make me Sick
6. Provide Me with Sweets
7. Pardon My Sobbing
8. Pimples May Surface
9. Pass My Sweat pants

11. Plainly; Men Suck
12. Pack My Stuff
13. Potential Murder Suspect
14. Please Make me Slim
15. Pretty Mood Sensitive

MI5 Job Opening

For the final test, the MI5 agents took one of the men to a large metal door and handed him a gun.

"We must know that you will follow your instructions, no matter what the circumstances. Inside the room you will find your wife sitting in a chair. Kill her!" The man said, "You can't be serious, I could never shoot my wife." The agent replied, "Then you're not the right man for this job. Take your wife and go home."

The second man was given the same instructions. He took the gun and went into the room. All was quiet for about five minutes. The man came out with tears in his eyes, "I tried, but I can't kill my wife." The agent said, "You don't have what it takes. Take your wife and go home."

Finally, it was the woman's turn. She was given the same instructions, to kill her husband. She took the gun and went into the room. Shots were heard, one after another. They heard screaming, crashing, banging on the walls. After a few minutes, all was quiet. The door opened slowly and there stood the woman, wiping the sweat from her brow. "This gun is loaded with blanks!" she said, "I had to beat him to death with the chair."

The moral of the story:
Women are evil. Don't mess with them.

A Woman's Perfect Breakfast

She's sitting at the table with her gourmet coffee. Her son is on the cover of the *Frosties* box. Her daughter is on the cover of *Glamour*. Her boyfriend is on the cover of *Playgirl*. And her husband is on the back of the milk carton.

Baby Blues

In a recent fictional survey, 1,000 women over 40 were asked to pretend to be an Agony Aunt for a series of pretty standard questions about pregnancy, hormones and other women's issues. Here is a transcript of the most typical woman's responses, offering valuable insight into how the tested group felt on a daily basis…

Q: SHOULD I HAVE A BABY AFTER 35?
A: No, 35 children is enough.

Q: I'M TWO MONTHS PREGNANT NOW. WHEN WILL MY BABY MOVE?

A: With any luck, right after he finishes university.

Q: WHAT IS THE MOST RELIABLE METHOD TO DETERMINE A BABY'S SEX?

A: Childbirth.

Q: MY WIFE IS FIVE MONTHS PREGNANT AND SO MOODY THAT SOMETIMES SHE'S BORDERLINE IRRATIONAL.

A: So what's your question?

Q: MY MIDWIFE SAYS IT'S NOT PAIN THAT I'LL FEEL DURING LABOUR, BUT PRESSURE. IS SHE RIGHT?

A: Yes, in the same way that a tornado might be called an air current.

Q: WHEN IS THE BEST TIME TO GET AN EPIDURAL?

A: Right after you find out you're pregnant.

Q: IS THERE ANY REASON I HAVE TO BE IN THE DELIVERY ROOM WHILE MY WIFE IS IN LABOUR?

A: Not unless the word 'divorce' means anything to you.

Q: IS THERE ANYTHING SPECIFIC THAT I SHOULD AVOID WHILE RE-COVERING FROM CHILDBIRTH?

A: Yes, pregnancy.

Q: OUR BABY WAS BORN LAST WEEK. WHEN WILL MY WIFE BEGIN TO FEEL AND ACT NORMAL AGAIN?

A: When the kids are at university.

FACTOID

Did you know..?

A recent study concluded that gossiping is good for women as it increases their levels of the female hormone progesterone, which allows women to have better interpersonal relationships.

The Female Rules

It's a generally accepted fact that women throughout the world have clubbed together and come up with a series of rules that men should follow. If the men don't know the rules, that's their problem. Here are the official Female Rules.

1. The female makes the rules.

2. The rules are subject to change by the female at any time without prior notification.

3. No male can possibly know all the rules. Any attempts to document the rules are not permitted.

4. If the female suspects that the male may know some or all of the rules, she must immediately change some or all of the rules.

5. The female is never wrong.

6. If the female could possibly be considered wrong, it is because of a ridiculous misunderstanding that was the direct result of something the male did, said, did not do, or did not say.

7. If rule 6 is invoked, the male must apologize immediately for having been the cause of the misunderstanding without any clues from the female as to what he did to have caused the misunderstanding. See rule 13.

8. The female may change her mind at any time for any reason or no reason at all.

9. The male is never permitted to change his mind in any circumstances without the express written consent of the female which is given only in cases where the female wanted him to change his mind but gave no indication of that wish. See rules 6, 7, 12, and 13.

10. The female has the right to be angry or upset for any reason, real or imagined, at any time and in any circumstance which in her sole judgment she deems appropriate. The male is not to be given any sign of the root cause of the female's anger or sorrow. The female may, however, give false or misleading reasons to see if the male is paying attention. See rule 13.

11. The male must remain calm at all times, unless the female wants him to be angry or upset.

12. In no circumstances may the female give the male any clue or indication whether or why she wants him to be angry or upset.

13. The male is expected to read the mind of the female at all times. Failure to do so will result in punishments and penalties imposed at the sole discretion of the female in question.

14. The female may, at any time and for any reason, resurrect any past incident without regard to temporal or spatial distance, and modify, enlarge, embellish, of wholly reconstruct it in order to demonstrate to the male that he is now or has in the past been wrong, insensitive, pig-headed, dense, deceitful, and/or oafish.

15. The female may use her interpretation of any past occurrence to illustrate the ways in which the male has failed to accord her the consideration, respect, devotion, or material possessions he has bestowed on other females, domestic pets or farm animals, sports teams, automobiles, motorcycles, boats, aircraft, or colleagues. Such illustrations are non-rebuttable.

16. If the female is experiencing PMS, Post-PMS, or Pre-PMS, the female is permitted to exhibit any manner of behaviour she wishes without regard to logical consistency or accepted norms of human behaviour.

17. Any act, deed, word, expression, statement, utterance, thought, opinion, or belief by the male is subject to the sole, subjective interpretation of the female, other external factors notwithstanding. Alibis, excuses, explanations, defences, reasons, extenuations, or rationalizations will not be entertained. Abject pleas for mercy and forgiveness are acceptable in some circumstances, especially when accompanied by tangible evidence of contrition.

Oestrogen Issue Rules

The most important thing for men to know, aside from the basic *Female Rules,* is the sub-set of *Oestrogen Issue Rules.* And it's worthwhile knowing them. Here are 10 ways to know if a woman has oestrogen issues:

1. Everyone around said female has an attitude problem.
2. She's adding chocolate to her cheese omelette.
3. The dryer has shrunk every last pair of her jeans.
4. Her husband is suddenly agreeing to everything she says.
5. She's using her mobile to call up every car sticker that says: "How's my driving? Call – "
6. To her, everyone's head looks like an invitation to batting practice.
7. Everyone but her seems to have just landed here from "outer space".
8. She can't believe they don't make Tampax bigger than Super Plus.
9. She's sure that everyone is plotting to drive her mad.
10. The Ibuprofen bottle is empty and she only bought it yesterday.

The Vicious "Men'strual" Cycle

A recent scientific study concluded that women find different male faces attractive depending on where the women are in their menstrual cycle. For example, when a woman is ovulating she will prefer a man with rugged, masculine features. However, when she is menstruating, she prefers a man with a cricket stump shoved up his backside.

When suffering from PMS and their periods, women will often go off men entirely, blaming men for never having to suffer like they do, and they will often hold little anti-men pow-wows with their female friends, laughing at arguably weak jokes such as:

Q: HOW DO YOU GET A MAN TO STOP BITING HIS NAILS?
A: Make him wear shoes.

Q: WHY DO MEN BECOME SMARTER DURING SEX?
A: Because they are plugged into a genius.

Q: WHY DON'T WOMEN BLINK DURING SEX?
A: They don't have enough time.

Q: WHY DOES IT TAKE ONE MILLION SPERM TO FERTILIZE ONE EGG?
A: They don't stop to ask directions.

Q: WHY DO MEN SNORE WHEN THEY LIE ON THEIR BACKS, LEGS APART?
A: Because their balls fall over their anus and they vapour lock.

Q: WHY WERE MEN GIVEN LARGER BRAINS THAN DOGS?
A: So they won't hump women's legs at parties.

Q: WHY DID GOD PUT MEN ON EARTH?

A: Because a vibrator can't mow the lawn.

Q: WHY DO ONLY 10% OF MEN MAKE IT TO HEAVEN?

A: Because if they all went, it would be Hell.

FACTOIDS

Did you know..?

- *70% of women cannot orgasm through vaginal intercourse alone*

- *At least 15% of the female population is capable of multiple orgasms*

- *When a woman is aroused her breasts swell by up to 25%*

- *Orgasms are good for you as they release endorphins*

The Hormone Hostage

At certain times of the month, women would rather fall in chocolate than fall in love. Learn the signs and just get them the chocolate. And don't think you're being kind by reminding the woman in your life that chocolate makes you fat. When under the influence of a chocolate moment she won't care, but she might scream at you.

The Hormone Hostage knows that there are days in the month when all a man has to do is open his mouth and he takes his life in his own hands! On the next page is a handy guide that should be as common as a driver's licence in the wallet of every husband, boyfriend, or significant other!

COMMENT RATING

1	=	DANGEROUS
2	=	SAFER
3	=	SAFEST
4	=	ULTRA SAFE

COMMENT	RATING
What's for dinner?	1
Can I help you with dinner?	2
Where would you like to go for dinner?	3
Here, have some chocolate	4

COMMENT	RATING
Are you wearing that?	1
Wow, you sure look good in brown!	2
WOW! Look at you!	3
Here, have some chocolate	4

COMMENT	RATING
What are you so worked up about?	1
Could we be overreacting?	2
Here are my wages	3
Here, have some chocolate	4

COMMENT	RATING
Should you be eating that?	1
You know, there are apples in the fridge	2
Can I get you a glass of wine with that?	3
Here, have some chocolate	4

COMMENT	RATING
So what did you do all day?	1
I hope you didn't overdo it today	2
I've always loved you in that robe!	3
Here, have some more chocolate	4

Top Ten Things Only Women Understand

There are just some things that men may never ever get and it's best just to take it as read that only women understand these things:

10. Cats' facial expressions.
9.   The need for the same style of shoes in different colours.
8.   Why bean sprouts aren't just weeds.
7.   'Fat' clothes.
6.   Taking a car trip without trying to beat your best time.
5.   The difference between beige, ecru, cream, off-white, and eggshell.
4.   Cutting your hair to make it grow.
3.   Eyelash curlers.
2.   The inaccuracy of all bathroom scales ever made.

AND, the Number One thing only women understand:

1.   OTHER WOMEN.

The Ideal Man

According to research, the Top 10 necessities of an ideal man, according to most women, are that he is:

1. Handsome.
2. Charming.
3. Financially successful.
4. A caring listener.
5. Witty.
6. Fit.
7. Stylish.
8. Appreciative of the finer things.
9. Full of thoughtful surprises.
10. An imaginative, romantic lover.

Female Musings

Some of the simplest things can set women off. Sometimes the daily stresses and strains of life have women asking themselves questions only to provide the answers, too. A way for them to hear what they want to hear? Sometimes it's just a matter of musings or sudden revelations to previously pondered theories or mysteries. Here are a few examples of the things a woman might find herself thinking or saying out loud to friends and, for men, they might offer an insight into the workings of the female mind…

- *Women over 50 don't have babies because they would put them down and forget where they left them*
- *One of life's mysteries is how a 2lb box of chocolates can make a woman gain 5lbs*
- *My mind not only wanders, it sometimes leaves completely*
- *The best way to forget your troubles is to wear tight shoes*
- *The nice part about living in a small town is that when you don't know what you are doing, someone else does*

- *The older you get, the tougher it is to lose weight because by then, your body and your fat are really good friends*

- *Just when I was getting used to yesterday, along came today*

- *Sometimes I think I understand everything, and then I regain consciousness*

- *I gave up jogging for my health when my thighs kept rubbing together and setting fire to my knickers*

- *It's important to note that every seven minutes of every day, someone in an aerobics class pulls a hamstring*

- *Amazing! You hang something in your closet for a while and it shrinks two sizes!*

- *Skinny people irritate me! Especially when they say things like... "You know, sometimes I forget to eat!" Now... I've forgotten my address, my mother's maiden name and my keys. But I have never forgotten to eat!*

- *A friend of mine confused her Valium with her birth control pills. She has fourteen kids but doesn't really care*

- *My body is not all that communicative but I heard from it the other day after I said, "Body, how would you like to go to the six o'clock class of vigorous toning?" Clear as a bell my body said, "Listen, witch... do it and die."*

- *The trouble with some women is that they get all excited about nothing and then they marry him*
- *I read this article that said that the typical symptoms of stress are eating too much, impulse buying and driving too fast. Are they kidding? That's my idea of a perfect day!*

The Pick of the Crop

Women are like apples on trees: the best ones are at the top of the tree. Most men won't reach for these good ones because they are lazy or afraid of falling and getting hurt. Instead they sometimes take the apples from the ground that aren't as good, but are easy.

The apples at the top of the tree begin to think something is wrong with them when in actual fact they are amazing; they just have to wait for the right man to come along.

Men are like fine wine: they begin as grapes and it's left to women to stomp the shit out of them until they turn into something acceptable to have dinner with…

A poem for girls…

I shave my legs
I sit down to pee
I can justify practically any shopping spree
Don't go to a barber, just a beauty salon
I can get a massage without getting a hard-on
I can balance a chequebook
I can fill my own car
Can talk to my friends about the size of my ar--
My beauty's a masterpiece and yes, it takes long
At least I can admit to others when I'm wrong
I don't drive in circles, at any cost
And I don't have a problem admitting I'm lost
I never forget an important date

You've just got to deal with it, I'm usually late
I don't watch films with a lot of gore
Don't need rewind to remember the score
I won't lose my hair, I won't get jock itch
And just 'cause I'm assertive, don't call me a bitch!
Don't say to your friends, Oh yeah, I can get her
In your dreams, my dear, 'cause I can do better!
Flowers are okay
But jewellery is best
Look at me, doofus...
Not at my chest!
I don't have a problem
Expressing my feelings
I know when you're lying
You look at the ceiling
Don't call me a girlie
a babe or a chick
I am a woman
So don't take the mick!

FACTOIDS

Did you know..?

- *The origin of the English word 'orgasm' derives from the Greek 'orgaein' meaning 'to swell' or 'be excited or lustful'*

- *The average person spends two weeks of their life kissing*

- *The French kiss is also known as the Soul Kiss because the life and soul were once thought to be exchanged through the sharing of breath*

- *Supposedly, the sexiest on-screen kiss was between Clark Gable and Vivien Leigh in Gone With The Wind. In reality the relationship wasn't so hot and she accused him of having bad breath*

THE FOOD OF LOVE

Scientists have discovered a food that diminishes a woman's sex drive by 90% … it's called a wedding cake.

"I love thee like a pudding, if thou wert pie I'd eat thee"
John Bray

"In the fifties, good girls didn't have sex; today good girls don't have chocolate"
Jeremy Iggers

"Food has replaced my sex life; now I can't get into my own pants"
Anon

"For women the best aphrodisiacs are words. The G-spot is in the ears. He who looks for it below there is wasting his time"
Isabel Allende

Feeding has always been closely linked with courtship. Remember those cavemen trundling home with an ancient beast on their shoulders and a couple of boulders between their thighs? Sadly, guys, it has been scientifically proven that women are more attracted to those of you who pick up the tab, which labels you as a good provider. If that's not your style, then why not cook for her? Modern girls are extremely impressed by a guy who cooks, an indication to them that you do not see them tied to the kitchen sink. But the last laugh is on her: you cooked, she washes up.

And girls, the old adage that the way to a man's heart is through his stomach isn't quite dead and buried. Although lots of guys like to cook these days, a girl who can whip up a good fry-up for breakfast plus a delicious Sunday roast, or who can organize a successful dinner party, still scores highly with many men.

Women like to be romanced and treasured, wined and dined. If a man were to cook her a meal at home, all the better. Candleight, Champagne, soft music, home-cooked food, prepared with care and attention, etc. are all guaranteed to put a woman at ease. Chocolate is always a favourite, no matter what the time or place. The aphrodisiac of all women and once upon a time kings! It has even been banned (and not because people were dieting). Casanova was a serious chocoholic – no wonder he could not wait to get into a girl's Snickers.

It goes without saying that a romantic meal means no burgers, no Ready Meals, no belching or farting, no Liebfraumilch or cheap lager. Instead think smart restaurants, cosy cafés, candlelit dinners (in the kitchen will do), sensual spooning of Häagen-Dazs into each other's mouths, or food straight from the fridge à la Kim Basinger and Mickey Rourke in *9 1/2 Weeks*.

"If music be the food of love, let's have a Beethoven butty"
John Lennon

Love Songs

Top songs to go with the wining and dining are:
Love Me Tender - Elvis Presley
I Will Always Love You - Whitney Houston
(Everything I Do) I Do It For You - Bryan Adams
Lady In Red - Chris De Burgh
I Just Called to Say I Love You - Stevie Wonder
How Deep is Your Love - Bee Gees
Be My Baby - from *Dirty Dancing*
Wonderful Tonight - Eric Clapton
When A Man Loves Woman - Percy Sledge
Groovy Kind Of Love - Phil Collins

Love Foods

Chocolate aside, top of the love food charts are:

- Asparagus
- Almonds
- Avocado (literally 'testicles' in ancient Aztec speak)
- Bananas (the fruit Eve was really after)
- Chilli
- Carrots
- Figs (Cleopatra's favourite)

- Grapes
- Mustard (a folklore remedy for impotence)
- Oysters
- Pine nuts
- Raspberries
- Shellfish
- Strawberries
- Truffles...

Simply Irresistible

A man is walking down the beach and comes across an old bottle. He picks it up, pulls out the cork and out pops a genie. The genie say, "Thank you so much for freeing me from the bottle. In return I will grant you three wishes."

The man says, "Great. I always dreamt of this and I know exactly what I want. First, I want a billion pounds in a Swiss bank account."

Poof! There is a flash of light and a piece of paper with account numbers appears in his hand.

He continues, "Next, I want a brand new red Ferrari right here." Poof! There is a flash of light and a bright red brand new Ferrari appears right next to him.

He continues, "Finally, I want to be irresistible to women." Poof! There is a flash of light and he turns into a box of chocolates.

Twenty Reasons Why Chocolate Is Better Than Sex

1. You can get chocolate very easily.
2. 'Swallowing' has real meaning with chocolate.
3. Chocolate satisfies even when it has gone soft.
4. You can have chocolate while you are driving.
5. You can make chocolate last as long as you want it to.
6. You can have chocolate in front of your parents.

7. You can bite the nuts if you like.

8. Two same-sex people can have chocolate without being called nasty names.

9. The word 'commitment' doesn't scare off chocolate.

10. You can have chocolate at your desk during work hours without upsetting your colleagues.

11. It's quite acceptable to have chocolate on your own.

12. You don't get hairs in your mouth with chocolate.

13. With chocolate there's no need to fake it.

14. Chocolate doesn't make you pregnant.

15. You can have chocolate any time of the month.

16. Good chocolate is easy to find.

17. You can have as many kinds of chocolate as you can handle.

18. You are never too young or too old for chocolate.

19. Having chocolate does not disturb your neighbours.

20. With chocolate size doesn't matter.

Foodie Valentine

Cabbage always has a heart
Green beans just string along
You're such a plum tomato
Will you peas to me belong?

You've been the apple of my eye
You know how much I care
So lettuce get together, dear
We'd make a perfect pear

Now something's sure to turnip
To prove you can't be beet
So if you carrot all for me
Let's allow our tulips meet

Don't squash my hopes and dreams now
Please bee my honey, dear
Or tears will fill potato's eyes
While sweet corn lends an ear

I'll cauliflower shop and say then
Your dreams are parsley mine
I'll work and share my celery
So be my Valentine

"You have to remember all the trivia that your girlfriend tells you, because eventually you get tested. She'll go: 'What's my favourite flower?' And you murmur to yourself: 'Shit, I wasn't listening... Self-raising?'"
Addy Van-Der-Borgh

CHAPTER 4:

Accepting the difference

"Women need a reason to have sex. Men just need a place"
Billy Crystal

"Women should be obscene and not heard"
Groucho Marx

"Women want mediocre men, and men are working hard to become as mediocre as possible"
Margaret Mead

"I hate women because they always know where things are"
James Thurber

"I always say shopping is cheaper than a psychiatrist"
Tammy Faye Bakker

Fairy Nuff

A fairy told a married couple: "For being such an exemplary married couple for 35 years, I will give you each a wish."

"I want to travel around the world with my dearest husband," said the wife. The fairy moved her magic stick and abracadabra! two tickets appeared in her hands.

Now it was the husband's turn. He thought for a moment and said, "Well this moment is very romantic, but an opportunity like this only occurs once in a lifetime. So... I'm sorry, my love, but my wish is to have a wife 30 years younger than me." The wife was deeply disappointed but, a wish was a wish. The fairy made a circle with her magic stick and... abracadabra!... suddenly the husband was 90 years old.

The moral of the story:
Men might be bastards but fairies are female!

Coming or Going?

A young man moved into a new flat on his own, and went to the lobby to put his name on his letterbox. Whilst he was there, an attractive young lady came out of the flat next to the letterboxes, wearing only a robe. The boy smiled at the young woman and she started a conversation with him. As they talked, her robe slipped open, and it was obvious that she had nothing else on at all. The poor kid broke into a sweat trying to maintain eye contact. After a few minutes, she placed her hand on his arm and said, "Let's go to my flat, I hear someone coming..."

He followed her into her flat; she closed the door and leaned against it, allowing her robe to fall off completely. Now nude, she purred at him, "What would you say is my best feature?" Flustered and embarrassed, he finally squeaked, "It's got to be your ears!" Astounded, and a little hurt she asked, "My ears? Look at these breasts, they are full and 100% natural! I work out every day! My backside is firm and solid! Look at my skin! No blemishes anywhere! How can you think that the best part of my body is my ears?!" Clearing his throat, he stammered, "Outside, when you said you heard someone coming? ...That was me."

FACTOID

Did you know..?
Over 50% of people fantasize more often about money than sex.

Money Talks

Still living at home and expecting to inherit a fortune when his sickly, widower father died, Robert decided he needed a woman to enjoy it with. So he went to a singles bar and he searched until he spotted a woman whose beauty took his breath away.

"Right now, I'm just an ordinary man," he said, walking up to her, "but within a month or two, my father will die and I'll inherit over 20 million pounds."

The woman went home with Robert, and four days later she became his stepmother.

The moral of the story:
Men will never learn!

"I love being married. It's so great to find that one special person you want to annoy for the rest of your life"
Rita Rudner

FACTOID

Did you know..?
It would take a typical couple more than four years to try every one of the positions described in the Kama Sutra.

Geography

Geography of Women

Between 18 and 22, a woman is like Africa:
half discovered, half wild, naturally beautiful with fertile soil.

Between 23 and 30, a woman is like Europe:
well developed and open to trade, especially for someone with cash.

Between 31 and 35, a woman is like India:
very hot, relaxed and convinced of her own beauty.

Between 36 and 40, a woman is like France:
gently aging but still warm and a desirable place to visit.

Between 41 and 50, a woman is like Great Britain:
with a glorious and all conquering past.

Between 51 and 60, a woman is like the former Yugoslavia:
having lost the war and haunted by past mistakes.

Between 61 and 70, a woman is like Russia:
very wide with borders now unpatrolled.

After 70, she becomes like Tibet:
*wildly beautiful, with a mysterious past and the wisdom of the ages...
only those with an adventurous spirit and a thirst for spiritual knowledge
visit there.*

Geography of Men

Between 1 and 70, a man is like the USA:
normally governed by a dick.

TO SUM UP

So to recap on the differences between the sexes, here's a quick reminder...

- Women are generally more sensitive to others' emotional pain than men are.

  Men are not mind readers, no matter how much women want them to be!

- Women are naturally interested in what others are thinking and feeling, and how others view them.

  Men can be fearful of expressing too much – if they really open up, will their women think them weak? Will they be rejected, feel humiliated?

- Women will often read things into a situation that aren't there.

  Men generally don't try and second-guess. They don't like arguing. They just want to know what's wrong so that they can try and fix it.

- If a woman talks to her man about a problem in her life, she's looking to share it – she's not complaining or asking him to sort it out. She's merely wanting him to listen and sympathize. He is a sounding-board, an ear; not expected to offer practical solutions.

  If a man talks to a woman about a problem, he generally wants some advice.

- Women are attracted to a combination of things in a man: good looks, mystery, confidence, competence, power, fun, sensitivity, intelligence, coolness, passion, understanding, patience, impulsiveness, and humour.

  Men are attracted to a pretty smiley face, a good figure, a sense of fun and humour and an easy-going nature. And long hair. They just are.

- A woman will take her time getting ready.

  Men expect women to be ready when they come to collect.

- A woman wants to feel cherished and protected.

  Being respected can often be more important to a man than being loved.

- A woman would, ideally, like about 30 minutes of foreplay.

  A man considers getting undressed as part of the foreplay.

- A 25-year-old woman tends to function as such.

  A 25-year-old man will still think it's hilarious to give a mate a wedgie after footie practice.

- A woman will buy thoughtful notelets and 'thank you' cards, even in this age of email. Occasionally she may dot her 'i's' with circles and hearts or put a smiley face at the end of a note.

  Men will chicken-scratch only when absolutely necessary.

- A woman will have many items in the bathroom ranging from the essential razor, shower gel, shampoo and conditioner, body cream, make-up remover, toothbrush and toothpaste through the needed but not necessarily essential hot oil hair conditioner, face mask, bath bomb etc. to the luxurious items most men would not be able to identify.

  A man has at most ten items in his bathroom, including a toothbrush, toothpaste, shaving cream, razor, bar of soap, and a towel.

- A woman will make a shopping list of things she needs and she will then go and buy these items, plus several things that have caught her attention along the way.

   A man will wait until the only items left in his fridge are half a lemon and something mouldy. Then he will go shopping and buy stuff that looks good. When his trolley is full he will go to the 10-items-or-less aisle. And get away with it.

- A woman may or may not love cats.

   A man may say he loves cats but when women are not looking he will kick cats.

And if that weren't enough, to finish up, here's a typical example of the difference between men and women and it goes a long way to explaining why men fart and women pick flowers:

Woman's Diary Entry

Saw him in the evening and he was acting really strangely. I had been shopping in the afternoon with the girls and I did turn up a bit late so thought it might be that.

The bar was really crowded and loud so I suggested we go somewhere quieter to talk. He was still very subdued and distracted so I suggested we go somewhere nice to eat.

All through dinner he just didn't seem himself; he hardly laughed and didn't seem to be paying any attention to me or to what I was saying. I just knew that something was wrong. He dropped me back home and I wondered if he was going to come in; he hesitated but followed.

I asked him again if there was something the matter but he just half shook his head and turned the television on.

After about 10 minutes of silence, I said I was going upstairs to bed.

I put my arms around him and told him that I loved him deeply. He just gave a sigh and a sad sort of smile. He didn't follow me up then but later he did, and I was surprised when we made love. He still seemed distant and a bit cold, and I started to think that he was going to leave me and that he had found someone else.

I cried myself to sleep.

Man's Diary Entry

England lost to South Africa. Gutted. Got a shag though.

~ THE END ~